DISCOVER SCIENCE

POLAR LANDS

 KINGFISHER

First published in 2012 by Kingfisher
This edition published 2017 by Kingfisher
an imprint of Macmillan Children's Books
20 New Wharf Road, London N1 9RR
Associated companies throughout the world
www.panmacmillan.com

ISBN 978-0-7534-4145-9

First published as *Kingfisher Young Knowledge: Polar Lands* in 2005
Additional material produced for Macmillan Children's Books by Discovery Books Ltd
Cover design: Wildpixel Ltd

Printed in China

9 8 7 6 5 4 3 2 1
1TR/0517/UTD/WKT/128MA

A CIP catalogue record for this book is available from the British Library.

Note to readers: the website addresses listed in this book are correct at the time of going to print.
However, due to the ever-changing nature of the internet, website addresses and content can
change. Websites can contain links that are unsuitable for children. The publisher cannot be held
responsible for changes in website addresses or content, or for information obtained through
a third party. We strongly advise that internet searches be supervised by an adult.

Acknowledgements
The publisher would like to thank the following for permission to reproduce their material.
b = bottom, *c* = centre, *l* = left, *t* = top, *r* = right

Photographs: cover: iStock; 1 iStock/axily; 2–3 iStock/jamenpercy; 4–5 iStock/Dmitry Deshevykh; 6–7 iStock/
MOF; 8–9 Corbis/Tom Bean; 8 SPL/Ted Kinsman; 9 Corbis Ralph A. Clevenger; 10–11 Corbis/Rob Howard;
11tr Getty NGS; 11br Corbis/Darrell Gulin; 12–13 Darrell Gulin; 13tr SPL/Simon Fraser; 13b Corbis/Charles
Mauzy; 14–15 Corbis/Dan Guravich; 14b Getty/Doug Allan; 15tr Corbis/Kennan Ward; 15cr Naturepl/Tom
Vezo; 16–17 B&C Alexander/Arctic Photos; 17br Corbis/Paul A. Souders; 18 Getty; 19tl B&C Alexander/Arctic
Photos; 19br Naturepl/David Pike; 20–21 Corbis/Alaska Stock; 21t Corbis/Tim Davis; 21c Natural History
Picture Agency/Laurie Campbell, Seapics, Hawaii, USA; 24–25 B&C Alexander/Arctic Photos;
24b Getty/Stone; 25b Naturepl /Doc White; 26t Corbis W. Perry Conway; 26b Corbis/Dennis Johnson, Papilio;
27 B&C Alexander/Arctic Photos; 28 B&C Alexander/Arctic Photos; 29tr SPL/Doug Allan; 29bl Ardea/Edwin
Mickleburgh; 30–31 B&C Alexander/Arctic Photos; 31t Corbis/Galen Rowell; 32 B&C Alexander/Arctic Photos;
33tl B&C Alexander/Arctic Photos; 33b B&C Alexander/Arctic Photos; 34 B&C Alexander/Arctic Photos;
35t B&C Alexander/Arctic Photos; 35 Getty/Popperfoto; 36 iStock/nevereverro; 37tl B&C Alexander/Arctic
Photos; 37–38 B&C Alexander/Arctic Photos; 38–39 B&C Alexander/Arctic Photos; 39tl SPL/David Vaughan;
39b B&C Alexander/ Arctic Photos; 40–41 Corbis/Dan Guravich; 41t Corbis/Wolfgang Kaehler; 41 Corbis/Tom
Brakefield; 48 iStock/Kenneth Canning; 49t Shutterstock/Vladimir Melnik; 49b Shutterstock/Andreas Gradin;
52 Shutterstock/dotweb; 53t Shutterstock/Gentoo Multimedia Ltd; 53b Shutterstock/Jorg Hackerman;
56 Shutterstock/Jan Martin Will

Commissioned photography on pages 42–47 by Andy Crawford
Thank you to models Harrison Nagle, Joley Theodoulou and Hayley Sapsford.

POLAR LANDS

Margaret Hynes

KINGFISHER

Contents

Ends of the Earth

North Pole

South Pole

The polar lands are found at the opposite ends of the world, in the far north and south, around the poles. They are the coldest and windiest places on Earth.

Frozen landscape

It is so cold in the polar regions that the land and sea stay frozen for most of the year. Polar animals need to be very tough to survive these conditions.

Adélie penguins

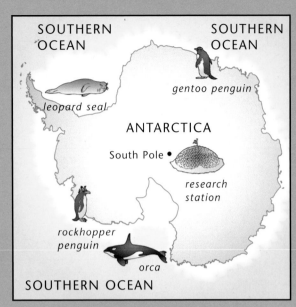

Arctic

The Arctic surrounds the North Pole. It is made up of the Arctic Ocean and the treeless lands around it, called the tundra.

Antarctic

The Antarctic surrounds the South Pole. It is made up of a continent called Antarctica, and the Southern Ocean around it.

Frozen features

It is so cold in the polar lands in winter that snow does not melt. Instead, it is pressed into ice as more snow falls on top of it. The ice forms thick sheets that cover the land.

Snowflakes

If you look closely at snowflakes, you will see they have many different patterns. Almost all snowflakes have six sides or six points.

Underwater giants

Icebergs are massive chunks of freshwater ice that float in the polar seas. The biggest part of an iceberg lies below the surface of the water.

Crashing ice

Icebergs break off the edge of polar ice sheets and crash into the sea. This mostly happens during the summer, when the ice melts a little.

Light and dark

The polar lands are unique places. During the long, harsh winters it is dark for almost the whole day. In summer, the Sun does not set for weeks on end.

Lighting the way

In the summer, the Sun dips in the sky at night, but it still lights up the land. Even though it is past midnight, these people can find their way home.

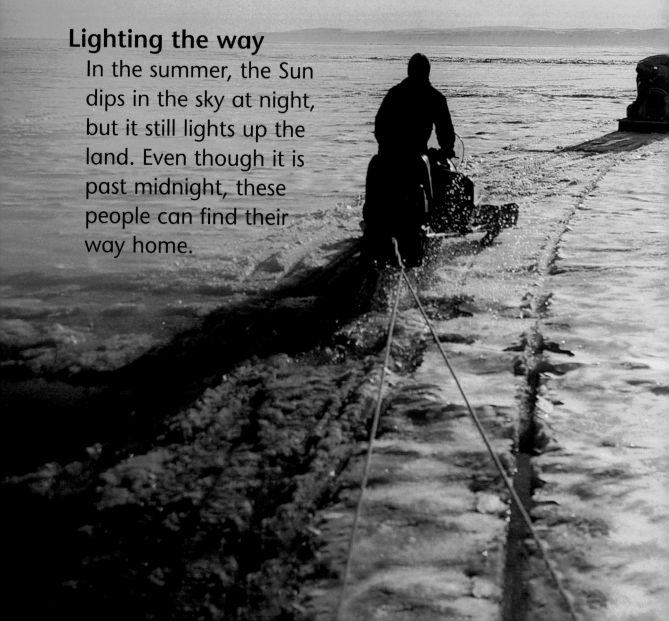

Strange lights

Near the poles, the night skies are sometimes filled with glorious light shows. These spectacular natural displays are called auroras, or the northern and southern lights.

Summer squirrelling

The ground squirrel survives the winter by hibernating. In summer, it makes the most of the constant daylight to gather a store of food for the next winter.

Tundra in bloom

The tundra is a cold plain that is covered with snow in winter. When the snow melts in summer, the tundra comes alive with flowers and animals.

Flowering carpet

A carpet of grasses, mosses and lichens covers the tundra in summer. These plants grow close to the ground, avoiding the freezing winds that howl above them.

Making seeds in the Sun

In the short summer, tundra flowers such as this Arctic poppy quickly blossom and produce seeds. Then the seeds lie frozen in the soil all winter.

Dining alone

Lone grizzly bears roam the tundra when it is in bloom. They feed on mammals, insects and plants, getting as fat as possible before the winter, when they hibernate in a den.

Adaptable animals

Animals that spend the winter in polar lands are specially adapted to survive in freezing temperatures. Many also have white coats so that they cannot be spotted in the snowy landscape.

Anti-freeze

This Antarctic ice fish survives in waters where most other fish would freeze solid. It has special chemicals in its body that stop it from freezing.

Changing coats

In winter, the ptarmigan grows thick white feathers for extra warmth and camouflage in the snow. In spring, it turns brown.

ptarmigan – winter

ptarmigan – spring and summer

Survival of the fattest

There is no danger of this walrus getting cold. Like all sea mammals, it has a thick layer of blubber under its skin. This body fat keeps it warm.

Who eats what?

Like all animals, Arctic animals keep busy by finding food. Some eat plants, while others are predators. Most animals need to protect themselves from predators.

Protective parents
Musk oxen do not run away when Arctic wolves come near. Instead, the adults form a circle around their young, so the wolves cannot catch them.

Arctic food chain

Arctic wolves are the top predators in this food chain. They eat musk oxen, hares and lemmings, which in turn feed on grass and lichens.

eats — Arctic wolf — *eats*

musk ox — Arctic hare — lemming

eats — grass and lichens — *eats*

Bully bird

In Antarctica, the skua is an aggressive predator. It threatens penguins and steals their eggs.

King of the ice

The polar bear is the largest and most powerful hunter of the Arctic. Bears roam alone over long distances each day in search of seals to eat. They also catch fish with their sharp claws.

Surviving the cold

Polar bears spend most of their time on ice floes. They are also excellent swimmers, and can spend many hours in the freezing water. Oily fur and a layer of blubber keeps these bears warm.

Junk food

Polar bears can stray into towns to find food. Sometimes they visit rubbish dumps, where they may be poisoned or injured.

Mother care

Baby polar bears are called cubs. They are born in a warm, cosy den that their mother digs in the snow. They grow quickly on their mother's rich, fatty milk.

Long-distance travel

For many polar birds and mammals, winter in the Arctic is just too cold. These animals migrate south to warmer places, and return again in spring.

Nomads of the north

Caribou are a type of deer. In winter, they live in forests on the edge of the Arctic. In summer, they travel 1,000 kilometres north to spend the summer feeding on tundra plants.

Flying visits

Arctic terns fly further than other birds. Each year they fly from the Arctic to the Antarctic and back, seeing summer at both poles.

On the hoof

Caribou can walk on deep snow without sinking. This is because their wide, fur-fringed hooves act like snowshoes by spreading their weight.

Life in polar seas

Polar seas are cold, but not as cold and hard to live in as polar lands. The deep waters of the polar seas are teeming with sea creatures.

Antarctic sea floor

Colourful anemones, fan worms and starfish sit on the Antarctic seabed. Sea slaters and sea spiders creep along the floor.

shoaling fish

sea anemone

sea slater

Sea food

Many animals in polar seas, from tiny fish to large whales, feed on plankton. These are microscopic animals and plants that drift in the water.

fan worm

sea spiders (red and yellow)

starfish

Sea mammals

The polar seas are home to whales, seals, sea lions and walruses. These mammals have blubber to keep them warm, and streamlined bodies that help them to move through the water easily.

Making a splash

Whales, such as this humpback whale, swim in the icy polar waters. They leap in the air and fall back into the water with a splash. This is called breaching.

Changing coats

Harp seals are born with fluffy white coats. The mothers take care of their babies for about two weeks, then the pups grow grey adult coats and must look after themselves.

Tusk tools

Walruses drag themselves out of the water using their tusks as levers. They also use their tusks to dislodge shellfish on the seabed.

albatross

Flying **squad**

Many seabirds spend summer at the poles. Most live on land, flying out over the sea and diving to catch food. The albatross stays at sea for most of the time, only coming ashore to lay its eggs.

Pointy eggs

Guillemots lay their eggs on cliff ledges. The eggs are pointed at one end. If they are nudged, they spin in a circle and do not fall off the cliff.

Cliff colonies

Puffins make their nests high up on cliffs so that predators cannot reach them. They breed in large, noisy groups called colonies.

Crowds of penguins

Penguins live in the coastal areas of the Antarctic. These birds cannot fly, but they use their wings to glide underwater as they chase their food.

Group hug

These young emperor penguins are huddling together to keep warm. They take turns to go in the middle, where it is warmest.

Sliding along

To travel quickly on land, Adélie penguins slide over the snow on their tummies. They use their wings to push and steer.

Feet off the ground

The ice is much too cold for young chicks. To keep off it, they stand on their mum's or dad's feet and snuggle under a special flap of skin on the adult's belly.

Inuit people

The Inuit people live in North America and Greenland. Traditionally, they travelled about in family groups and survived by fishing and hunting. Today, many Inuit live in towns.

Cosy icebox

When they are on hunting trips, Inuit people build igloos as temporary homes. Although they are made from frozen blocks of ice and loose snow, they are cosy and warm inside.

Boat sense

The Inuit are expert boat-builders. They cover their boats in sealskin, which keeps them watertight. This boat is an umiak.

A herder's life

Some Saami, Lapp and Chukchi people are herders. They follow wild reindeer herds and settle in camps wherever the reindeer stop to feed.

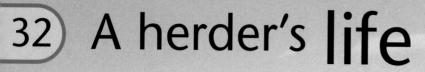

Reindeer power
Reindeer pull sleds and carry heavy loads and riders. They also provide meat, and skins for clothing and shelter.

Winter warmth

These men are wearing warm winter coats, called parkas, made from reindeer skin. The soft, warm fur is worn against the men's skin.

Mobile homes

Arctic herders move several times a year, so their homes have to be simple and light. They live in tents made from a cone-shaped wooden frame, covered with reindeer skins.

Polar exploration

Many explorers risked their lives trying to be the first people to set foot at the poles. In 1909, Robert Peary reached the North Pole. In 1911, Roald Amundsen beat Robert Scott in a race to the South Pole.

Modern-day explorers

Today's polar explorers wear layers of specially designed clothing to keep warm in freezing temperatures. They pull their supplies on lightweight sledges.

An explorer's best friends

Amundsen and his team learned
from Arctic people and used husky
dogs to pull their sledges. Huskies
are strong and intelligent, and
well adapted to the cold.

Over sea and land

Scott and Amundsen
sailed part of the way
to the South Pole. Once
they reached land, they
loaded their supplies onto
sledges and continued
their journeys on skis.

Scott's ship, the Terra Nova

Modern life

Improvements in transport, food, building and clothing have brought a modern way of life to the Arctic. Most people now live in small towns and work in modern industries.

Arctic towns

Arctic towns are like other small towns, except that water has to be delivered by truck. The water would freeze if it was distributed through pipes.

People carrier

The people living in polar lands no longer rely on animals for transport. Today, they travel on skidoos or snowmobiles – motorized sledges.

Oil industry

The Arctic's rich supplies of oil are processed in plants such as this one. Oil is one of the world's most important fuels and is used to make many goods. The oil industry provides jobs, but harms the Arctic environment.

Scientific research

The only people who live in Antarctica are scientists working in research stations. They study Antarctica's wildlife and find out about its climate.

Weather watching

Every day, scientists measure and record the weather conditions. The measuring instruments are attached to a balloon that floats 20 kilometres above ground.

Drilling for information

Using a special drill, scientists extract long samples of ice, called cores. The layers of ice have built up over thousands of years. Studying them helps scientists to learn about the Earth's past climate.

Animal tracking

A tag on this Weddell seal's tail helps scientists record when and where they see this particular seal. This helps us to learn more about seals' lives, and how to protect them.

Protecting wildlife

People have lived in the Arctic for thousands of years without harming the environment. Recently, though, people have endangered wildlife by hunting and by pollution.

Free ride home

Polar bears are quite rare, and most northern countries have laws to protect them. Bears that wander into towns are caught and airlifted back to the wild.

Watching and protecting

These tourists in Antarctica are on a carefully organized trip. This helps make sure that wildlife is not disturbed too much.

Saving sea mammals

Special sanctuaries in the Southern Ocean protect the feeding grounds of whales and orcas. Most countries have agreed not to hunt in these areas.

orca (killer whale)

Smart snowflakes

Make a paper snowflake

Real snowflakes have six sides or points, so you need to fold a piece of paper into six sections before you create a pattern.

Place the plate onto the white paper. Using a pencil, draw round the plate to make a circle. Then carefully cut out the circle shape.

You will need
- Plate
- White paper
- Pencil
- Scissors
- Coloured card (optional)
- Glue (optional)
- Glitter (optional)
- Shiny paper (optional)

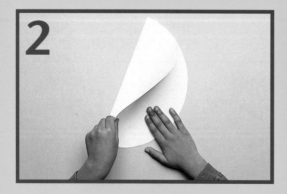

Use the white paper circle you have made to create your snowflake. Start by folding the circle in half to make a semi-circle.

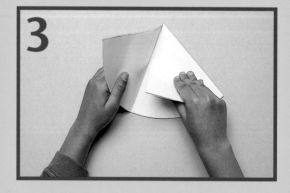

Fold the semi-circle into three equal parts, as shown, to make six sections. This means your snowflake will have six sides.

4

Draw a pattern on your folded paper. Make sure you do not draw right across the paper. You could start by copying this pattern.

5

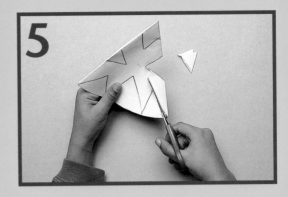

Cut away sections of the folded paper, following the pattern. Take care not to cut right across the width of the paper.

6

Unfold your snowflake carefully. You will see that the patterns on each of the six sections are identical – like a real snowflake!

Have fun making and displaying lots of snowflakes. You can glue your snowflakes onto coloured card and decorate them with glitter and shiny paper.

Ice fun!

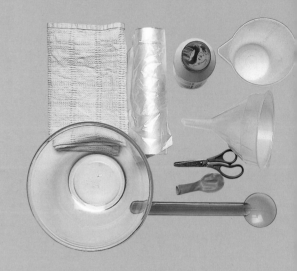

Incredible iceberg

An iceberg may take thousands
of years to form from layers and
layers of snow. You can make
your own iceberg overnight.

You will need
- Jug
- Water
- Balloon
- Funnel
- Plastic bag
- Freezer
- Clear bowl
- Tablespoon
- Salt
- Scissors
- Tea towel

1 Fill the jug with cold
tap water. Fit the
funnel into the neck
of the balloon and
hold it in place. Ask
an adult to help you
fill the balloon.

2 Ask an adult to tie the
end of the balloon to
seal the water inside.
Put the balloon inside
a plastic bag and
place in a freezer
overnight.

3 Next day, fill the
clear bowl three-
quarters full with
water. Then add
about 5 to 10
tablespoons of salt
to make seawater.

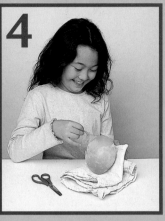

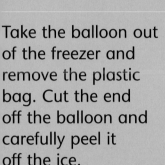

Take the balloon out of the freezer and remove the plastic bag. Cut the end off the balloon and carefully peel it off the ice.

Using a tea towel or cloth so that your fingers do not stick to the cold ice, carefully place your iceberg in the bowl of salty water.

Your iceberg will float in the salty water. You will see that only a small portion of the whole iceberg stays above the water's surface.

Penguin game

Play the penguin game and pretend to be a penguin keeping its egg safely above the cold ice.

You will need
- Bean bag

Penguins keep their eggs and babies safely above the ice by carrying them on their feet. To play the penguin game, you and a friend need to pass a bean bag 'egg' to each other without dropping it on the floor, using only your feet.

Penguin mask

Make a penguin face

Rockhoppers are small Antarctic penguins with brightly coloured faces. Make a penguin mask and you can look like one!

1

Start by tracing the rockhopper penguin template at the back of this book. Then transfer your tracing onto your piece of card.

You will need
- Tracing paper
- Pencil
- Black card
- Scissors
- Modelling clay
- Apron or overall
- Paint: red, yellow
- Elastic
- Glue
- Yellow tissue paper

2

Using the scissors, carefully cut out the shape of the penguin mask. You may want to ask an adult to help you with this.

3

Use a pencil and modelling clay to pierce holes for the elastic strap and for the eyeholes. Enlarge the eyeholes with scissors.

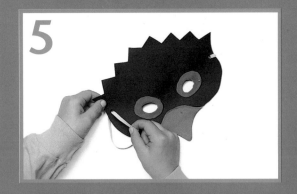

Wearing an apron or overall, paint your penguin mask. Use red for the eyes and orange for the beak. (Make orange paint by mixing red and yellow paint.)

When the paint is dry, cut a piece of elastic that is long enough to fit around your head. Tie the ends into each of the small holes on the side of the mask.

Cut two strips of yellow tissue paper. Spread a thin line of glue above the eyes, and glue on the strips of tissue paper to make the penguin's feathery eyebrows.

Have fun wearing your mask and pretending to be a rockhopper penguin.

Glossary

Auroras – natural night-time light displays that occur in the sky near the poles

Blossom – to produce flowers

Blubber – a layer of body fat beneath the skin of animals such as whales and seals that protects them from the cold

Breed – to produce babies

Camouflage – a shape, colour or pattern that helps hide an animal

Climate – usual weather conditions in one place over a period of time

Colony – a group of animals living together

Continent – one of the Earth's seven huge blocks of land

Environment – natural surroundings

Extract – to dig out

Food chain – a diagram that shows who eats what in a particular place

Freshwater – water that is fresh, like rain or river water, not salty like seawater

Glide – to move smoothly through water or air

Herders – people who look after herds of animals

Hibernating – spending the whole winter in a deep sleep

Ice floe – a large chunk of floating ice

Industries – businesses that make goods and sell them for money

Lichen – a mossy growth found on walls, rocks and trees

Lightweight – designed to weigh as little as possible

Mammal – a warm-blooded animal that feeds its young on milk

Melt – to change from snow or ice into water

Microscopic – much too small to be seen with the human eye

Migrate – to make a journey from one place to another every year, at the same season

Plain – a large, flat, mainly treeless area of land

Plankton – tiny animals and plants that live just below the surface of the ocean

Poles – the points furthest north and furthest south on Earth

Pollution – chemicals and other materials that damage the environment

Predator – an animal that hunts and eats other animals

Roam – to wander over a large area

Sanctuary – a place where animals are protected from danger

Seabird – a bird that lives near, and feeds from, the sea

Snowshoes – shoes for walking on snow, with a frame that is strapped to the foot

Streamlined – having a smooth body shape that moves easily through water

Steer – to guide in the right direction

Teeming – full of living creatures

Temporary – lasting for a short time

Tundra – a cold plain that is covered with snow in winter

Tusks – long teeth that poke out of an animal's mouth

Unique – not like any other

Watertight – describes something that keeps water out

Parent and teacher notes

This book includes material that would be particularly useful in helping to teach children aged 7–11. It covers many elements of the English and Science curricula and cross-curricular lessons especially those involving Geography and Art and Design.

Extension activities

Reading
Find all the mentions of the word 'hibernate'. What does it mean? Which polar animals hibernate, and which do not? Why do you think they are different?

Writing
Create a table showing the differences and similarities between the Arctic and Antarctic.

How do people live in the Arctic? How are some people using it? Are any of them changing it? Write a short report.

Write an explorer's diary with entries from all of the seasons, showing how polar regions change depending on the time of year.

Speaking and listening
Find out the different ways that animals move over the polar surface. Act them out to some of your friends and see if they can guess what action and animal you are mimicking.

Science
This book is about the topic of habitats. It also includes links to the themes of animal life cycles and behaviour (pp11, 13, 14–15, 16–17, 18–19, 20–21, 22–23, 24–25, 26–27, 28–29), Earth (pp6–7, 10–11), keeping warm (pp14–15, 30, 33), solids and liquids (pp8–9, 36) and environmental issues (pp36–37, 38–39, 40–41).

Find as many things as you can that help animals survive the polar cold, such as blubber. You can present your information in a table – list the animal and what helps it to survive.

...ross-curricular links

...esign: Read about the caribou's ...owshoes on page 21, and ...ok at the picture of the people ...earing snowshoes on page 33. ...esign a pair of snowshoes that ...ould help to spread your weight ...n the snow.

...ok at the sleds on pages 32, ...4–35. Design a sled that could ...arry supplies across the Arctic. ...hink about the materials that ...ou need to build it and what ...ape you need to make it ...) that it is easy to pull over ...ong distances.

...sing the projects

...hildren can follow or adapt these ...rojects at home. Here are some ...deas for extending them:

...ages 42–43: Can you decorate ...) Christmas card with a paper ...nowflake on it? Try using tissue ...aper. Or make two identical ...ard snowflakes, then cut a slot ...) each from the side to the centre ...nd fit them together to make a ...-D snowflake.

Pages 44–45: Make it a prize iceberg by adding small, waterproof toys to the water. You and your friends can chip away at the ice to get a prize.

Page 45: Measure how far you and your friends can walk with the bean bag on your feet. Change the game and use an orange instead of a bean bag – it is much harder!

Pages 46–47: Make a mask for another polar animal, too. You could make a seal, a polar bear or a walrus.

Did you know?

- Polar bears are so adapted to living on ice that they don't need to drink. They get all of the water they need from the prey that they eat.

- The world's largest ever snowflake fell in 1887 in Fort Keogh, Montana, USA and measured 38 centimetres wide and 20 centimetres thick.

- Female grizzly bears usually give birth to twins. The cubs stay with their mother until they are around 2 years old, when they go and fend for themselves.

- The Inuit call musk oxen 'Oomingmak', which means 'animal with skin like a beard'.

- When there is nothing to eat on the tundra, caribou scrape snow away from rocks with their feet or antlers and eat lichens and small shrubs.

- When Roald Amundsen reached the South Pole in 1911, he left a letter for Robert Scott. Just four weeks later, Scott found the letter, which said he could help himself to a sledge and other supplies Amundsen had left.

- Richard Byrd was one of the first people to fly over the South Pole. His crew had to dump most of their supplies just to get over the Transantarctic mountains. If they had broken down, they wouldn't have been able to continue on foot.

- Adélie penguins are named after the wife of a French explorer. They make their nests using stones, and sometimes fight over the best ones.

- Polar bears have short ears and tails so that they don't lose too much body heat from them.

Once albatrosses leave their nests they may not return to land again for seven to ten years.

When hunting, polar bears wait quietly near a hole on the sea ice for a seal to surface, before grabbing it with their sharp teeth.

When a penguin chick hatches, it starts calling to its parents immediately. This is so that the parents recognize their chick by its call when they come back with food.

Caribou can travel up to 5,000 kilometres on their long migration to the Arctic.

- Adult albatrosses have been recorded to fly almost 900 kilometres a day.

- Walruses can slow their heartbeats to withstand the temperatures of their surrounding waters. This means that they can stay under water for as long as ten minutes.

- Long ago some people thought that the northern and southern lights (auroras) were souls or spirits dancing in the sky.

- The array of colours that appear in the northern and southern lights consist of red, blue, violet and green.

Polar lands quiz

The answers to these questions can all be found by looking back through the book. See how many you get right. You can check your answers on page 56.

1) Where does the biggest part of an iceberg lie?
   A – Above the water
   B – Below the water
   C – Neither above or below the water; they are equal

2) What is the name given to the ice that scientists extract to study climate?
   A – Ice bores
   B – Ice cores
   C – Ice floes

3) What do polar bears usually eat?
   A – Fish and seals
   B – Birds
   C – Trees and plants

4) What do people do with polar bears that wander into towns?
   A – Catch them and airlift them back to the wild
   B – Catch them and put them into sanctuaries
   C – Catch them and keep them in zoos

5) How do penguin chicks keep warm?
   A – They stand on their parents' feet
   B – They run around
   C – They swim

6) What shape are the guillemot bird's eggs?
   A – Oval
   B – Round
   C – Pointed at one end

7) What do musk oxen do to protect their young from wolves?
   A – Charge at the wolves
   B – Find shelter for their young
   C – Form a circle around their young

8) What do Arctic herders use to keep warm?
   A – Coats made from sealskin
   B – Coats made from reindeer skin
   C – Coats made from polar bear skin

9) What do explorers use to help them get around and pull their sledges?
   A – Arctic wolves
   B – St Bernard dogs
   C – Husky dogs

10) How many sides or points does a snowflake usually have?
    A – 8
    B – 6
    C – 5

11) What do walruses use their tusks for?
    A – To eat
    B – To pull themselves out of the water
    C – To help them swim

12) What are the colour of a ptarmigan's feathers in winter?
    A – Brown
    B – White
    C – Black

Find out more

Books to read

Antarctica by Lucy Bowman, Usborne Publishing, 2007

Arctic Wildlife Nature Activity Book by James Kavanagh, Waterford Press, 2011

Freezing Poles (It's all about...) Kingfisher, 2015

Polar Lands (In Focus) Kingfisher, 2017

The Arctic (Animal Homes) by Holly Duhig, Book Life, 2017

What Lives in the Arctic? by Oona Gaarder-Juntti, Super Sandcastle, 2008

Places to visit

Highlands Wildlife Park, Kincraig, Scotland

www.highlandwildlifepark.org

Visit this exciting wildlife park and you can take a peek at Walker, a two-year-old polar bear, and some of Scotland's breathtaking wildlife.

London Zoo

www.zsl.org/zsl-london-zoo/exhibits/penguins/

Visit the Penguin Beach exhibit at London Zoo and watch these amazing animals as they dart and dive about in the water. There are some great underwater viewing tunnels so you can see the penguins twist and turn. You can even meet the penguins and watch them being fed.

The Polar Museum, Scott Polar Research Institute, Cambridge

www.spri.cam.ac.uk/museum

Visit this amazing museum to find out about polar history and exploration. View some unique artefacts, including Arctic material from the indigenous peoples of Canada, Greenland and Alaska, photos and artworks, maps, clothing and much more.

Websites

http://wwf.panda.org/about_our_earth/ecoregions/about/habitat_types/habitats/polar_regions/

Find out all about the polar regions in this section of the World Wildlife Fund's website. There is also a useful section on polar animal life.

www.nationalgeographic.com/polarexploration/explore-poles.html

Visit this website to find out about the weather in the Arctic and Antarctic regions. There are some great facts about these regions, as well as fantastic pictures of the animals that live there.

www.bbc.co.uk/nature/habitats/Polar_region

You can view some amazing video clips on this BBC website. Witness the Arctic melt and the Antarctic freeze before you, as well as the spectacular southern lights and the harsh conditions faced by Weddell seals in the Antarctic.

Polar lands
quiz answers

1) B	7) C
2) B	8) B
3) A	9) C
4) A	10) B
5) A	11) B
6) C	12) B